W9-BHE-238

Usborne Bible Tales
MOSES
IN THE
BULRUSHES

Retold by Heather Amery

Illustrated by Norman Young
Designed by Maria Wheatley

Language consultant: Betty Root
Series editor: Jenny Tyler

This is baby Moses.

He is just three months old. He was born in Egypt
a very long time ago.

Moses' parents were Hebrews.

The Egyptians made the Hebrews work very hard building cities and temples.

This is the King of Egypt.

He was a cruel man. He was afraid the Hebrews would not obey the people of Egypt.

"The baby boys must die."

The King ordered his soldiers to find all the Hebrew baby boys and kill them.

Moses' mother decided to hide her son.

"Please don't cry," she said. She was afraid the Egyptian soldiers would find him and kill him.

She took her baby to the river.

Moses' mother went to the Nile. She cut down lots of bulrushes and made them into a big basket.

She put Moses in the basket.

She kissed him and put the basket down on the water. The basket floated away.

Moses' sister was on the river bank.

She watched the basket. She followed it as it floated down the river.

Moses was asleep in the basket.

It floated past the Princess of Egypt. She was bathing in the water with her maids.

The Princess saw the basket.

"What's that?" she said. "Bring it here."
One of the maids picked up the basket.

The Princess looked at Moses.

Moses woke up and cried. "What a lovely baby,"
said the Princess. "He must be a Hebrew boy."

Moses' sister ran to the Princess.

"Do you want a Hebrew nurse for the baby?" she said. "Yes, bring one to me," said the Princess.

Moses' sister went to get her mother.

"Look after this baby," said the Princess. "I will pay you well." Moses' mother took him home.

Moses was safe.

He grew up with his own family. When he was old
enough, his mother took him back to the Princess.

"He's my son now," said the Princess.

Moses lived in the palace like an Egyptian prince.
But he never forgot he was a Hebrew.

This edition first published in 2003 by Usborne Publishing Ltd, 83-85 Saffron Hill, London EC1N 8RT, England. www.usborne.com
Copyright © 2003, 1996 Usborne Publishing Ltd.
The name Usborne and the devices 🔔 🌐 are Trade Marks of Usborne Publishing Ltd. All rights reserved. No part of this publication may be reproduced, stored in a retrieval system, or transmitted in any form or by any means, electronic, mechanical, photocopying, recording or otherwise, without prior permission of the publisher. UE. This edition first published in America in 2003. Printed in Belgium.